BOG MUMMIES

by
Joyce Markovics

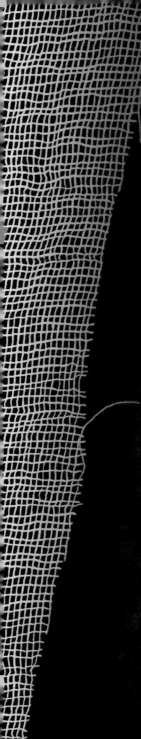

CHERRY LAKE PRESS

Published in the United States of America by Cherry Lake Publishing Group
Ann Arbor, Michigan
www.cherrylakepublishing.com

Reading Adviser: Marla Conn, MS Ed., Literacy specialist, Read-Ability, Inc.
Content Adviser: Owen Beattie, PhD
Book Designer: Ed Morgan

Photo Credits: Wikimedia Commons and © Malte Pott/Shutterstock, cover and title page; Wikimedia Commons, TOC; © flickr, Lindy Buckley, 4–5; © DrimaFilm/Shutterstock, 4; © Ian Dagnall/Alamy Stock Photo, 5; © Niels Bach, 6; Wikimedia Commons, 7; Wikimedia Commons, 8; Wikimedia Commons, 9; © dpa picture alliance archive/Alamy Stock Photo, 10; Wikimedia Commons, 11; Wikimedia Commons, 12; Wikimedia Commons, 13; © fotoaway/Shutterstock, 14 bottom; Wikimedia Commons, 14 top; Wikimedia Commons, 15; Wikimedia Commons, 16–17; Wikimedia Commons, 18–19; © SomprasongWittayanupakorn/Shutterstock, 19 top; © Florida Historical Society/*Life and Death at Windover: Excavations of a 7,000-Year-Old Pond Cemetery* by Rachel K. Wentz, 20; © Florida Historical Society/*Life and Death at Windover: Excavations of a 7,000-Year-Old Pond Cemetery* by Rachel K. Wentz, 21.

Cherry Lake Press is an imprint of Cherry Lake Publishing Group.

Library of Congress Cataloging-in-Publication Data

Names: Markovics, Joyce L., author.
Title: Bog mummies / by Joyce L Markovics.
Description: Ann Arbor, Michigan : Cherry Lake Publishing, [2021] | Series:
   Unwrapped: marvelous mummies | Includes bibliographical references and
   index. | Audience: Ages 8 | Audience: Grades 2-3
Identifiers: LCCN 2020030272 (print) | LCCN 2020030273 (ebook) | ISBN
   9781534180406 (hardcover) | ISBN 9781534182110 (paperback) | ISBN
   9781534183124 (ebook) | ISBN 9781534181410 (pdf)
Subjects: LCSH: Bog bodies—Juvenile literature.
Classification: LCC GN293 .M352 2021 (print) | LCC GN293 (ebook) | DDC
   393/.3—dc23
LC record available at https://lccn.loc.gov/2020030272
LC ebook record available at https://lccn.loc.gov/2020030273

Printed in the United States of America
Corporate Graphics

CONTENTS

A DARK DISCOVERY 4

BOG BODIES 8

DEEP IN PEAT 12

AMERICAN BOG PEOPLE 18

Mummy Map 22
Glossary 23
Find Out More 24
Index 24
About the Author 24

A DARK DISCOVERY

On May 8, 1950, the police in Silkeborg, Denmark, got a shocking call. Nearby, some farmers had found a male body in a peat bog. The dead man looked as if he had recently died. And, more upsetting, he had a rope around his neck. Had the man been strangled or hanged?

This is a peat bog. Farmers dig up and cut the peat to use as fuel.

The police rushed to the bog. When they saw the body, they could tell it was old. The farmers had actually dug up a 2,400-year-old bog mummy!

The dead body was found under nearly 7 feet (2 meters) of peat. It was curled up like a sleeping child.

A mummy is a dead body that has been preserved in some way.

The policemen and villagers carefully packed the bog body in a crate. Then it was shipped to a museum. There, **archaeologists** excitedly examined every part of it. They named the body Tollund Man.

This illustration shows Tollund Man being moved in a crate. How did he get his name? Two of the farmers who found him came from the village of Tollund.

Parts of Tollund Man were perfectly preserved. Scientists could see wrinkles on his forehead. They even saw eyelashes, pores, and a very short beard on his face. When they looked inside Tollund Man's stomach, they found grains from his last meal!

A smooth leather cap covered Tollund Man's short hair.

Experts think Tollund Man was hanged to death. He was around 40 years old when he died.

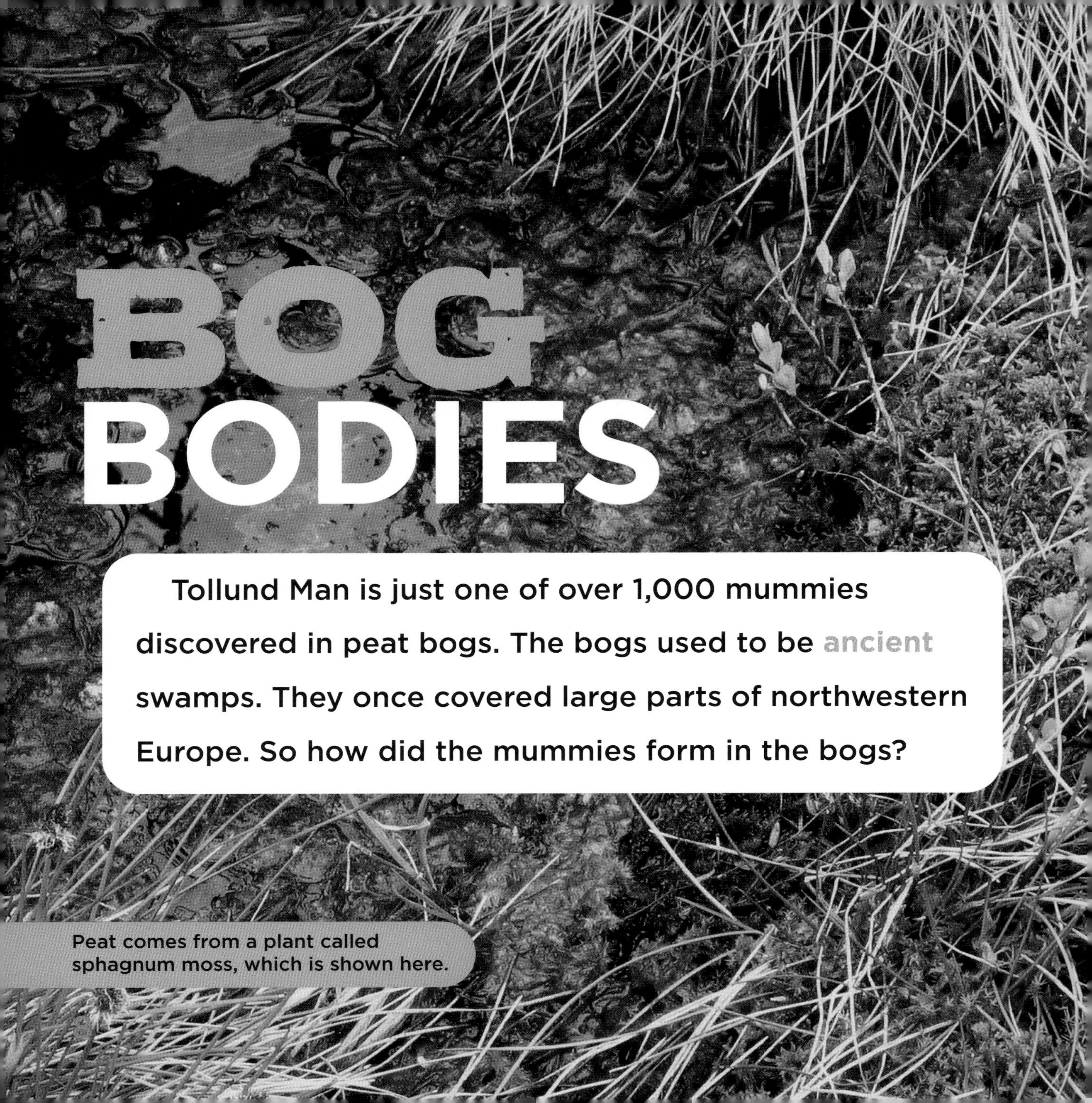

BOG BODIES

Tollund Man is just one of over 1,000 mummies discovered in peat bogs. The bogs used to be ancient swamps. They once covered large parts of northwestern Europe. So how did the mummies form in the bogs?

Peat comes from a plant called sphagnum moss, which is shown here.

Bacteria are tiny living things that help break down dead bodies. Few bacteria can survive in bogs. This, in turn, slows decay. The bogs also contain a special kind of acid. This chemical preserves the bodies. And it makes skin leathery and dark in color.

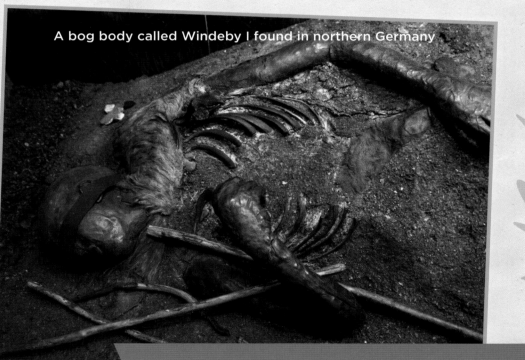
A bog body called Windeby I found in northern Germany

Bog bodies are often very well preserved. Scientist Karin Frei says they look like they will open their eyes and start talking!

By studying bog mummies, scientists uncovered a dark secret. Many of the bodies show signs of **violence**. Some of them were strangled or hanged, like Tollund Man. Others were stabbed or beaten to death. Then their bodies were thrown into bogs.

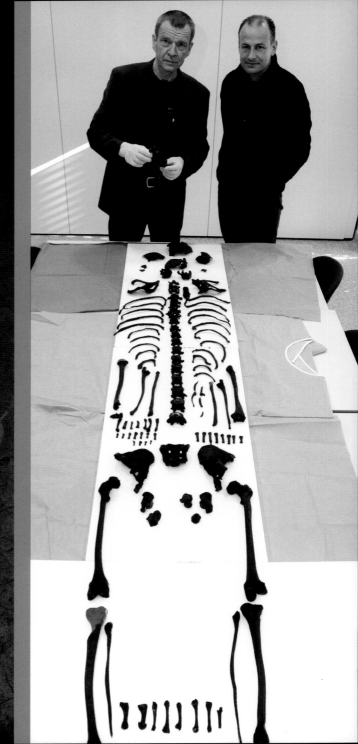

Sometimes, only bones are found preserved in a bog. Here, scientists examine the skeleton of a bog mummy named Bernie.

No one knows why the people were killed. However, ancient records provide a clue. Many of the mummies may have been criminals and put to death for their crimes. Experts also think that some were human sacrifices.

This bog mummy has a large hole in his head. Experts think he was beaten to death.

Long ago, people sometimes made human sacrifices to their gods. This may have been done to thank the gods or ask for help.

DEEP IN PEAT

Another famous bog mummy is Yde (EE-dah) Girl. In 1897, villagers from Yde, the Netherlands, found the girl under layers of peat. Her body was nearly 2,000 years old. She was wrapped in a wool cape and had very long hair. Before Yde Girl was dumped in the bog, she was likely strangled.

Experts think Yde Girl was 16 years old at the time of her death.

In 1992, after examining Yde Girl, scientists made a lifelike model of her head. Today, people can view the head at a Dutch museum. And they can gaze into the eyes of a girl from over a century ago!

A model that shows what Yde Girl's face might have looked like

Half of Yde Girl's head was shaved. Experts believe this was punishment for something she may have done before she died.

In 1952, a farmer discovered a bog body in Denmark. He was collecting peat when he struck something. "I stood on the shovel, and it wobbled," said the farmer. He got down on his knees to see what it was. It was a human head!

The head was deformed from being buried for so long.

The body the farmer found was later named Grauballe Man. It was more than 2,000 years old. Grauballe Man would become one of the most studied bog mummies of all time!

Grauballe Man's hands were well preserved. So scientists fingerprinted him. His fingerprint is one of the oldest on record!

Who was Grauballe Man? Archaeologist Peter Glob led the investigation. By looking at the skeleton, Peter learned that Grauballe Man was about 35 years old when he died. His teeth were badly worn. And he had parasites. But the ancient man was in pretty good health.

The bog mummy was buried without any clothing.

What was unusual was that Grauballe Man's throat had been cut from ear to ear. Because of this, Peter believes the ancient man was a human sacrifice.

Peter looked inside Grauballe Man's body. He found vegetable soup in the mummy's stomach!

AMERICAN BOG PEOPLE

The site of Windover Pond where the bones were found

Bog bodies aren't just found in Europe. In 1982, workers were digging near Windover Pond in Florida. All of a sudden, their backhoe hit something hard. When they looked down, they saw human bones.

Archaeologists were called in to collect and test the bones. The results were surprising. The bones were over 7,000 years old. This was thousands of years older than most bog bodies! Soon after, the pond was drained and the exploration began.

Archaeologists found 168 burials at the Windover site. Many of the bodies were in a seated pose. Some were staked to the ground to keep them from floating to the top of the pond. Most of the remains were bones. However, over half of the skulls found still contained brains!

The team of experts who explored the Windover Pond site

Many artifacts were also uncovered. The team found handmade fabrics and tools. By studying them, experts learned how the early people of Florida lived and died.

A drawing showing how the bodies might have been staked

Experts think the Windover site was used as a burial ground. Half of the bodies were female, and half were male. Their ages varied from young to old.

MUMMY MAP

Grauballe Man
About 100 BCE to 100 CE
Aarhus, Denmark

Yde Girl
About 100 BCE to 50 CE
Yde, the Netherlands

Tollund Man
About 400 BCE
Silkeborg, Denmark

Windover Pond Mummies
About 6000 to 5000 BCE
Florida, United States